YOGA

*

A Guide to
Healthy Living

YOGA
A Guide to Healthy Living

Text:

S. K. Sharma
Balmukand Singh

BARNES
&NOBLE
BOOKS
NEW YORK

© Lustre Press Pvt. Ltd. 1998
Third Impression, 2000

This edition published by
Barnes & Noble, Inc.
by arrangement with
Lustre Press

2000 Barnes & Noble Books

M 1 0 9 8 7 6 5 4 3

ISBN: 0-7607-1250-6

Yogasanas
by :
Balmukand Singh
Padma Sakha

Authors:
S. K. Sharma
Balmukand Singh

Acknowledgements
We wish to acknowledge with
gratitude the help extended to us by
the Central Research Institute for
Yoga, Delhi, and the Department of
Indian Systems of Medicine,
Ministry of Health and Family
Welfare, Government of India.

Photography:
Deepak Budhraja

Processed at
Laser Graphics Pvt. Ltd.,
New Delhi

Printed and bound by:
Star Standard Industries Pte. Ltd.,
Singapore

Text Editor:
Bela Butalia

Production:
N. K. Nigam, Abhijeet Raha

Conceived & Designed by:
Pramod Kapoor
at
ROLI CAD CENTRE

The Meaning
of Yoga
7

The Asanas
11

Yoga
for
Everyday Fitness
13

Yoga Therapy
71

Pranayama
79

Dhyana
81

THE MEANING OF YOGA

Yoga, which has been practised in India for over two millennia, is becoming increasingly popular and relevant for people today. It is a philosophy, a science and an art, in short a way of life. Yoga leads to physical, mental, emotional and spiritual development. With its holistic understanding of the individual in the macrocosm, yoga offers a person a total approach to help cope with the stress of modern life.

The term yoga is derived from the word *yuj* in Sanskrit. *Yuj* means to join. Yoga is that which joins. According to the traditional yoga texts, the entities which are joined by *yuj* are the individual self *(jivatma)*, with the universal self *(paramatma)*. This implies that every aspect of a human being, from the innermost to the external must be integrated.

In yoga philosophy the body is made up of a series of five sheaths,

Men do not know themselves and have not learned to distinguish the different parts of their being; for these are usually lumped together by them as mind. Yoga helps us to become conscious of the great complexity of our nature, and the different forces that move it.

Lights on Yoga
—Sri Aurobindo

one superimposed on the other. The outermost, physical sheath *(annamaya kosa)* is nourished by the food we eat. The vital sheath *(pranamaya kosa)* refers to the air we breathe and without which there is no life. The astral sheath *(manomaya kosa)* refers to the coordinating functions of the brain. The wisdom sheath *(vijnamaya kosa)* aids us in discriminating and exercising our free will. The fifth sheath, the *anandmaya kosa*, is the consciousness which links a person with the universal consciousness. An awareness of this complexity by itself helps a person to feel that he is a part of an immense whole rather than an isolated unit.

The secret of yoga is the achievement of a sense of balance and control: control on the body, breath and mind. Apart from the atoms which make up our gross physical body, we possess breath

(*prana*), mind, intellect, emotions and spiritual dimensions. The body's stamina has to be developed, the breath should be balanced, the mind calmed, the emotions stabilized, the intellect held under control and the mind made one with the self or *atma*. The practice of physical postures (*asanas*), entailing physical exercise and breathing techniques are the means by which to achieve this control which is essential to lead a worthy and satisfying life.

Knowledge about yoga predates the oldest Indian scriptures, called the Vedas. Further, elaboration about yoga is found in the holy books of the Upanishads and their commentaries in the Puranas, and in the epics (the *Ramayana,* and the *Mahabharata)*, the latter containing the famous *Bhagavad Gita.* But it is the great sage Patanjali from the pre-Christian era who is considered to be the propounder of yoga philosophy. The author of works on medicine, grammar and yoga, he took the essential features and principles of yoga indicated in the Upanishads and compiled them in his *Yoga Sutras.* The *Yoga Sutras* is still considered an authoritative text today. It summarizes all the various aspects of yoga.

According to Patanjali, yoga consists of eight steps or 'limbs' (*angas*) which are interrelated. These are:

1. The Five Abstinences (*yamas*), which are best expressed as positives instead of negatives: non-violence, truthfulness, non-stealing, continence and non-covetousness.
2. The Five Observances or *niyamas*: purity, contentment, mortification (or austerity) study and resignation to God.
3. Practice of postures or *asanas*. Regular and devoted practice of various postures of yoga to promote physical fitness and slow relaxation.
4. Practise of breath control (*pranayama*).
5. Sense-withdrawal (*pratyahara*): by this practice the mind gradually withdraws from the objects perceived through the senses.
6. Concentration (*dharana*): the practise of focusing the mind on some object which is unmoving.
7. Concentration or meditation (*dhyana*): the mind is made one with the object it contemplates, and a quiet, meditative state is developed.
8. Intuitive enlightenment or state of bliss (*samadhi*): This step leads to full integration or absorption of the individual with the essence of the object contemplated, or with the divine.

All these steps are successive stages on the path of yoga, the ultimate aim being self-realisation. Yoga, though a part of Hindu philosophy, is not a religion. Though advocating liberation, yoga employs an approach which utilises psycho-physiological techniques and controls. Hence whatever the metaphysics behind the aim of yoga, there is no doubt that practical benefits accrue on many levels from the practise of yoga. In other words, people of any religious faith or belief can practise yoga and experience true peace of mind.

  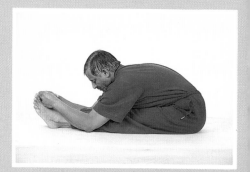

  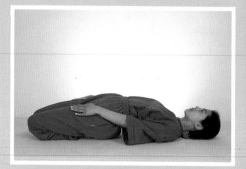

THE ASANAS

A Way Towards General Well-being

The practice of *asanas* is the third of the eight steps indicated earlier which leads to the highest stage of yoga philosophy, namely, meditation. The Indian texts mention 8,400,000 *asanas*, but generally about hundred *asanas* are practised in different conditions. One of the classic yoga texts, the *Hatha Yoga Pradipika*, defines the use of *asanas* as poses to be practised for gaining 'steady posture, health and lightness of body'.

The word *asana* literally means seat. Originally, it referred to the pose in which the saints sat in meditation, but now the word has come to be associated with all yogic postures. Meant to be sustained for a given duration of time, the postures encompass a number of lying, supine, standing, sitting, twisting, prone, inverted and balancing positions. Based on

'Yogasanas *are to be practised in the manner a child grows. The new born is supine. A few months later he turns over on his stomach. Then he sits up and when a year old, he steadies himself on his feet and slowly starts to walk and run. Similarly, first asanas are practised lying on the back, to be followed by those to be done in face-down, sitting and then standing positions.'*

a deep understanding of the principal areas of control of the body, the *asanas* specifically focus on the spine, which keeps the body upright and provides the vital channel for the nervous system. Keeping the spine flexible and exercising the muscles of the trunk enhances suppleness, improves the functions of the digestive and abdominal organs and the endocrine glands. This makes for more effective breathing and calms the mind generally. The postures are meant to be relaxing and refreshing.

The *asanas* described here are listed in the order in which they appear in the classic texts like *Hatha Yoga Pradipika, Gheranda Samhita* and *Yoga Kundalyaopanishad.* They are categorized according to the increasing level of arduousness of the pose, from the beginning to the advanced, and keeping in view the ability of the practitioner. In the Central Institute for Yoga, Delhi, yoga classes start with simple *asanas*, to be followed by the more complicated ones, which are practised over a period of a month. Over forty *asanas* may be performed during the course of a single practise session, according to Balmukand Singh, yoga teacher at the institute.

In recent years, medical practitioners in India have come to recognize and accept the therapeutic value of specific *asanas* for treating specific ailments. These include bronchial asthama, heart ailments, diabetes, spondylosis, hypertension, migraine, depression, and eye-disorders, among others. The *asanas* may be used as a treatment in themselves, or as a supplement to other treatments.

Normally, persons of all ages, from seven to ninety, men and women alike, may practice *yogasanas*. If you have a special health condition, consult a doctor or a qualified yoga teacher before commencing a yoga course. Select an open, clean place or room, which is quiet, free of dust and fumes, and has an even temperature. Spread a thick sheet or carpet on the floor. Now you are ready to begin. Start practising gradually, a few *asanas* at a time. Begin with the *Shavasana* (page 24), which totally relaxes the body, and finish the practice session with the same *asana*. Relax between two *asanas*. Allow the breath to settle before starting the next *asana*. Avoid talking, laughing or questioning during the practice and be completely calm. Closing your eyes and concentrating on your breathing or on some symbol, like OM, or on God's image, enhances concentration.

YOGA
FOR EVERYDAY FITNESS

Guidelines for Practitioners

To be Observed	To be Avoided
❖ *Asanas* should be practised early in the mornings or in the evenings. In the mornings, face the rising sun while practising.	❖ Avoid practising if suffering from fever, diarrhoea or any other acute condition. During menstruation, *asanas* should not be practised. Pregnant women should only practice a few simple *asanas* under expert guidance (see stage XII of chapter 'Yoga Therapy').
❖ Practice *asanas* on an empty stomach. If your practice session is scheduled during the day or the evening, an interval of at least four hours should lapse after the last meal.	❖ You may feel a slight pain when you first start practising *asanas*. Do not worry, for within a week of regular practise the aches will disappear.
❖ Brush your teeth, empty your bladder and bowels, and have a bath before practising *asanas* in the early morning.	❖ Perform the *asanas* according to your *physical* capacities. Don't practise to the point of fatigue.
❖ Wear loose clothes during practice sessions. In India, men often wear minimum clothing, like swimming trunks, while practising *asanas*.	❖ If you perspire while practising, do not wipe off the perspiration, let it evaporate.
❖ If you suddenly feel like sneezing, coughing, passing stools or urinating, interrupt the practice session for a few minutes, ease yourself and then return to the practise.	❖ Spread a carpet/sheet on the floor and perform *asanas*. Avoid air-conditioned rooms. If the season permits perform *yogasanas* in the open, in the morning and evening.
❖ You can take food or milk approximately one hour after practice.	

Siddhasana

Perfect Posture

The *Siddhasana* is considered to be one of the main *asanas*. It may be practised daily. The word *siddha* means 'adept'; thus, *Siddhasana* is denoted by the name Perfect Posture. Yogis often sit in this pose while meditating.

1 Sit on the floor with the legs outstretched and apart. Place the heel of the left foot against the perinium, the soft flesh found between the genitals and the anus.

2 Place the right foot in a similar manner. The toes should be concealed between the thigh and calf muscles. The thighs and knees should rest flat on the ground. Alternate position of feet.

3 Place the hands lightly on the knees, palms facing upwards, with thumbs and forefingers put together to make a circle. Rest your gaze between the eyebrows.

Benefits:
This *asana* purifies the 72,000 channels of the body and enhances overall concentration. This posture is also useful in cases of anxiety, depression, insomnia and blood pressure.

Elderly people having osteo-arthritis of the knee-joints may have difficulty in doing this *asana* in the begining but regular practice can enable them to achieve this posture.

Padmasana

Lotus Posture

This is probably the best-known among the yoga *asanas* and may be performed by all with benefit. Also called the Buddha Posture, it is a meditation posture used to achieve the higher stages of yoga.

1 Sit on the floor. Pull each foot onto the opposite thigh and in against the groin, with the soles of the feet upturned.

2 The heels should be close together. The knees should touch the ground. Straighten the spine; the head and neck should be poised in line with it. Look straight ahead.

3 Rest the upturned palm of the right hand lightly in the left one, near the navel, or on the knees with the palms facing upwards; the thumb and index finger are held together in a circle.

Benefits:
Stimulates the digestive fire (*jathrangni*) and is particularly helpful in curing indigestion, poor appetite and constipation.

Elderly people might find it difficult to do this *asana* in the beginning. In such cases, just keep one leg straight, bring the heel of the other foot below the groin and gradually press the flexed knee to touch the floor.

Bhadrasana

Blessed Posture

Bhadrasana has been found useful for developing the ability to concentrate because the mere practise of fixing the gaze leads to stabilising the mind.

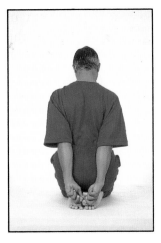

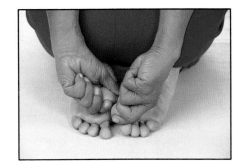

2 Hold the right toe with the left hand and the left toe with the right hand.

1 Kneel on the floor (the soles and heels should be together), and sit over the heels.

3 Keeping the back straight, flex the neck so that the chin touches the chest. Rest your gaze on the tip of the nose.

Benefits:
Useful for diseases of the neck, as it regulates the activities of the thyroid gland. Also strengthens the cervical area, toes, heels, calf-muscles and knees and enhances concentration.

Do not practice this *asana* if you are suffering from cervical spondylitis and neck pain of any kind. In case you do try, look straight ahead and do not bend your neck.

Muktasana

Liberated Posture

The *Muktasana* is similar to the *Siddhasana* (shown on page 15). For those who find the *Siddhasana* difficult, the *Muktasana* is an easier alternative.

1 Sit on the floor and flex the left knee so that the heel touches the anus.

2 Bring the right heel over the left leg without displacing your left heel.

3 Tuck your toes in-between the thighs and calves. Place the hands lightly on the knees, palms upturned. The spine and neck should be erect, the eyes looking straight ahead.

Benefits:
It has advantages similar to those achieved by performing the *Siddhasana*.

Vajrasana

Adamantine Posture

In this posture the vital energy flows upwards from below and gives the body great strength. It can be used for the practice of *pranayam* or breath control and for meditation. Many other *asanas* start with the *Vajrasana*.

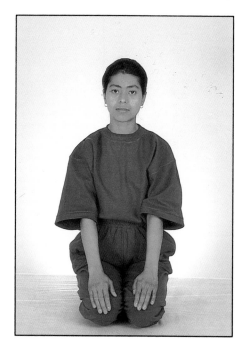

1 Kneel with your knees together. Keep the heels apart but interlock the big toes.

2 Sit on the heels keeping the back straight. The inner edges of the heels support the outer edges of the buttocks. Place the palms on the knees and look straight ahead. Hold the pose for 20-60 seconds.

Benefits:
Apart from aiding digestion, this *asana* also strengthens the knees, calves and thighs, making it useful for chronic ailments of the knee-joints. It also helps in problems relating to sleep.

Swastikasana

Swastik-type Posture

This posture can be counted among the *asanas* ideal for meditation. By practising this pose you gain a sense of stability and balance which helps to promote a feeling of self-mastery.

1 Sit cross-legged on the floor. Tuck the toes of the right foot between the calf and thigh muscles (behind the knee) of the left leg.

2 Similarly, tuck the toes of the left foot between the thigh and calf muscles of the right leg. The knees rest on the floor.

3 The heels should be kept away from the genitals. The hands rest lightly on the knees, palms upturned. The spine and neck are erect and the gaze is straight ahead.

Benefits:
Helps to overcome the feeling of excessive cold in the feet during winters. In India, this *asana* helps counter excessive perspiration and a feeling of excessive heat in the feet.

Simhasana

Lion Posture

Simh means lion. Highly regarded in yoga, this *asana* is so-called because practising it requires a person's tongue to be protruded, much like that of a lion!

1 Squat on the floor with knees outstretched. Flex the toes and join the lifted heels. Sit on them, so that they take the weight of the body.

2 Balance the body by placing your hands on the knees.

3 Straighten the spine, bend the neck so that the chin touches the chest. Now protrude the tongue down as far as is possible. The gaze should be on the tip of the nose.

Benefits:
Protruding of the tongue tones up the face and throat muscles and tonsils as well as improve eyesight. Helpful in preventing diseases of the gums and tonsils, the pose also broadens the chest.

Obese and plump persons, as also the elderly, should practice this *asana* gradually, with the support of some prop, like a wall.

Gomukhasana

Cowface Posture

Go means cow and *mukha* is face in Sanskrit. This pose resembles a cow's face when viewed from the back.

1 Sit on the floor as in *Vajrasana* (see page 19). Bend forward and raise the body, so its weight rests on the hands. Pass the right flexed knee over the left one.

2 Sit on the left heel, resting the body's weight on it. The soles face upwards.

Benefits:
As this *asana* expands the lungs, it is helpful for asthma, tuberculosis and other lung disorders, high blood pressure and mental strain. It is useful for piles and prostrate gland problems.

3 Bend the right arm, raising the elbow high. Stretch your hand over the right shoulder, as far down the middle of the back, keeping the spine erect.

4 Bring the left hand up the centre of the back from below so that the hands meet. The palm of the right hand faces the back and the palm of the left faces outwards. Look straight ahead.

Veerasana

Hero's Posture

This posture is considered a favourite of the two Hindu deities, Hanuman and Angada. Practised regularly, it is believed to help develop self-confidence.

1 Rest the right knee on the floor. Bend the left knee, so that the left foot is on the floor.

2 Bring the arms parallel to the shoulders; clench the fists.

3 Slowly straighten the right leg and raise the body so that its weight is on the left foot. Extend the left arm; flex the right arm so that the elbow touches the waist.

Benefits:
As this *asana* strengthens the legs and arms, it helps in problems related to tremors in the extremities caused by neuro-muscular diseases. It is also useful for regulating sleep.

Shavasana

Corpse Posture

This *asana* derives its name from *shava* which means corpse in Sanskrit. It is meant to be a total-relaxation posture for the body and mind.

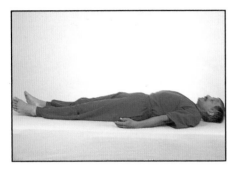

1 Lie on your back and relax all parts of your body from head to toe. Stretch the legs, so that the feet are relaxed, the toes a little apart and the heels together. The palms should face upwards, the fingers should be limp and slightly curled up. Close the eyes and relax the body for a few minutes.

VARIATION I

VARIATION II

Two variations to this pose are either by turning to one side or lying supine and listless on the belly. Concentrate on deep, gradual breathing.

> *Benefits:*
> As it rests the mind, this pose is useful for blood pressure, heart diseases, mental stress and strain, poor sleep, restlessness, anger and depression.

Gaurakshasana

Cowherd Posture

This *asana* is named after a great yogi called Gourakshnath.

1 Sit on the ground with legs outstretched. Join the heels and soles and bring them under the anus.

2 Both the feets should be joined together sole to sole. Sit on the heels.

3 Keep the hands in *gyan mudra* and look straight ahead.

Benefits:
Useful in urinary disorders and piles, this *asana* also helps to normalise blood pressure and aids in concentration. Also useful in leukorrhea, prolapse of the uterus and dismenorrhoea.

Utkatasana

Squatting Posture

The *Utkatasana* pose is considered to be one of the thirty-two main *asanas* in Hatha Yoga, and is used during some internal cleansing processes basic to yoga.

1 Squat on the ground keeping the feet parallel, the elbows on the knees, the fingers interlocked and the chin resting on the fingers.

2 Gradually, raise the heels and rest the body weight on the toes. Beginners may separate the toes and knees to maintain the balance.

Benefits:
Helps in problems relating to nocturnal discharge of semen, pain in the toes and heels. It also improves concentration and body balance.

Those suffering from prolapse of the uterus, piles, rectal prolapse, should not practice this *asana*.

Paschimottanasana

Posterior-stretch Posture

In Sanskrit, *paschima* means back and *tan* means to stretch; hence the term posterior or back-stretching posture. It may require quite some practice before the spine is supple enough to achieve the final pose.

1 Sit on the floor with legs stretched out together in front of you. Raise both your arms and take a deep breath.

2 Exhale, bend forward and grasp the toes if possible, or, alternatively, the ankles.

3 Try to bend as far forward as possible so that the forehead touches the knees.

Benefits:
Reduces abdominal fat, fights intestinal worms, improves digestion and functioning of the endocrine glands. Also counters pain in the joints, back and feet, and helps in skin diseases, diabetes, colitis and thyroid disturbances.

Those suffering from backache, cervical spondylitis or sciatica should avoid this *asana* in the initial stages of their yoga practise.

Sankatasana

Contracted Posture

Sankat literally means danger, but despite this name there is no danger involved in performing this *asana*!

1 Stand with your feet together. Your palms should hang beside your thighs. Shift your weight on the right foot and twist the left leg over the right leg.

2 Raise your arms, twist them while interlocking the fingers, and stretch yourself upwards.

3 The arms and legs should appear like strings intertwined to form a rope. Repeat the *asana* by standing on the left foot.

Benefits:
Helpful in diseases of the legs, the knees and the joints, this *asana* is useful for soldiers and guards who have to be on their feet for many hours, also helps prevent hydroceal.

Mayurasana

Peacock Posture

Considered among the advanced postures in yoga, this *asana* requires you to have strong arms and good coordination. It has many variations. The simplest version is given here.

1 Kneel. Rest the palms (fingers pointing towards the feet and spread out) on the floor in front of the knees. The toes should be separated. Leave 3-4 inches of space between the wrists.

2 Flex the elbows and bring the body weight forward on to the palms. Raise the body parallel to the ground. At first, keep the feet near the hips, so that both the feet and hands support each other.

3 When the body stabilises with practice the legs can be straightened so that the whole body is held parallel to the floor.

Benefits:
Useful in abdominal ailments, like disorders of the liver, spleen and gall-bladder, as also diabetes, constipation and indigestion. Purifies the blood and cures skin diseases.

Do not practice this *asana* if you suffer from high blood pressure, hernia or peptic ulcer.

Guptasana

Concealed Posture

The *Guptasana* resembles the *Siddhasana* (page 15). The position of the legs and ankles is, however, a little different.

1 Sit on the floor with the legs outstretched and the heels and toes together. Bend the left leg to bring the heel under the anus.

2 Bend the right leg, bringing the right heel over the left heel. Raise yourself a little on your hands, so as to be able to sit on the right heel.

3 Tuck the toes of the left foot under the right leg; keep the big toe out. The right foot should come under the *popliteal fossa* (depression at back of leg, behind knee). Rest hands on knees, palms upwards. Look straight ahead.

Benefits:
This pose improves the blood circulation in the genital organs and thereby corrects uro-genital disorders. Counters pain in the toes, ankle-joints and soles. Aids concentration.

Kukkutasana

Cock Posture

This pose is also considered to be among the advanced *asanas* in yoga. It should be attempted after a certain level of suppleness and coordination has been achieved.

1 Sit in *Padmasana* (see page 16).

2 Insert the left arm up to the elbow between the right foot and left calf, and the right arm up to the elbow between the right calf and thigh.

3 Spread your plams on the ground and lift your hips and body off the floor and rock forward so as to balance on the palms. Hold this position for some seconds.

Benefits:
Strengthens the arms and shoulders.

Matsyasana

Fish Posture

Practise this *asana* only on a coarse mat, otherwise you are likely to slip. It is so-called because one may actually be able to float in water like a fish while in this pose by spreading out the arms, though only after mastering the pose.

 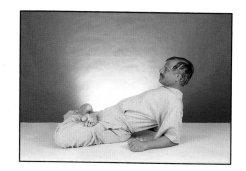 

1 Sit on the floor in *Padmasana* (see page 16).

2 Lie back on the floor, supporting yourself on your elbows, your hands close to the hips.

3 One by one straigthen your elbows so that you are lying down. Lie down so that your thighs, hips, back and head rest comfortably on the ground.

Benefits:
Helps in backache, lumbago and cervical spondylitis. It is useful for thyroid problems and bronchial asthma, besides regulating the menstrual cycle.

Matsyasana:

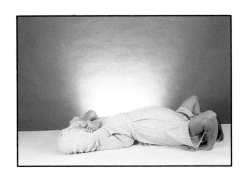

4 Inverting your palms, raise yourself on them from the shoulders upwards. Arch your trunk and throw back the head, pressing the crown on the floor.

5 The shoulders and back should be off the floor. Grasp your toes with the hands. The eyes should focus between the eyebrows.

Being an advanced *asana*, it should be practised only under expert guidance. Those suffering from peptic ulcer, ulcerative colitis, hernia, blood pressure and heart diseases should avoid performing this *asana*.

Matsyendrasana

Matsyendra Posture

This posture is named after Guru Matsyendranath, one of the founders of Hatha Yoga. Follow each step of this complex *asana* carefully, to be able to practice it properly.

1 Sit on the floor with legs outstretched. Flex right leg to bring the right heel near the umbilicus high on the left thigh.

2 Shift weight to sit on the right thigh, while supporting yourself with the hands stretched way back behind the buttocks.

3 Bring the left ankle and foot over the right flexed knee and place on the floor. The right foot will get raised off the floor.

> *Benefits:*
> Helps cure diseases of the liver, spleen, intestines and pancreas, besides being useful in diabetes and aiding digestion; helps to stabilise semen in the body.

Matsyendrasana:

 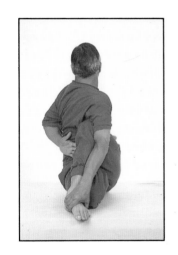 

4 Bring the right arm around the left knee and place on floor. The body weight rests on the right thigh, the left foot and the hands.

5 Hold the left foot with the right hand Bring left arm behind back. Body should be in a backward twist. Slowly twist the trunk leftwards so that the left hand is held across the lower back.

6 Reach out with the right arm so that the left knee goes behind the right armpit and grasp the left foot or ankle with the right hand. Keep the spine as straight as possible, and the gaze behind the left shoulder.

Kurmasana

Tortoise Posture

By sitting like a tortoise in this *asana*, you will be able to conserve your body heat for a long period. The practice of this asana is hence recommended.

1 Sit in *Vajrasana* (see page 19), clench the fists, placing your thumbs inside.

2 Unite the elbows and bring to the umbilicus. Bend forward and press the elbows against the thighs.

3 Your vision should rest between the eyebrows.

Benefits:
Affects the *nabhi-cakra* (near the navel), and corrects constipation and knee disorders. Useful in bronchial asthma and hernia. Aids concentration and respiration.

Vrikshasana

Tree Posture

This posture may be performed in several ways. The one described here belongs to the group of balancing postures.

1 Stand with your feet wide apart. Bend forward so that the hands/palms rest firmly on the ground. The hands should be about 1-1½ feet apart.

2 Raise the body gradually so that the weight of the body rests wholly on the palms. Straighten the legs upwards and unite the feet to balance each other.

Benefits:
Improves the blood circulation in the heart and brain, improves vision, and affects the pituitary and pineal glands. Also useful in sinusitis and skin diseases.

Beginners suffering from blood pressure, backache or heart diseases should not practice this *asana*, except under expert supervision.

Uttankurmasana

Stretched Tortoise Posture

The *Uttankurmasana* is among the eleven chosen *asanas* which are regarded as capable of bestowing supernatural powers on men. The *nabhi-cakra* or navel-plexus, believed to be the source of 72,000 nerves, can be regulated by this *asana*.

1 Sit in *Vajrasana* (see page 19), Lean back on your elbows, the palms on the ground behind the hips.

2 Tuck in the elbows one by one, so that the body rests on the feet and the shoulders.

3 Lower the head to the ground so that the body rests on the feet, the shoulders and the back of the head. Rest the hands on the thighs for some time.

Benefits:
As this *asana* strengthens the thighs and makes the spinal cord flexible it helps in problems of the heels, ankles and back. Also checks bronchial asthma and respiratory disorders.

Mandukasana

Frog Posture

Mandukasana or the Frog-posture is the name given to the *asana* in which the body is bent forward and the head slightly raised to resemble a frog.

1 Sit in *Vajrasana* (see page 19). Clench one fist and place it on the navel. Place the other hand over the first.

2 Bend forward as far as is possible so that the chest touches the knees.

3 Lift your head and look straight ahead.

> *Benefits:*
> Reduces external fat, regulates the functioning of bile and phlegm in the body, helps the digestion and improves vision; also conserves body energy. In the cold season one can warm up the body by sitting in this posture.

Garudasana

Eagle Posture

Garuda means an eagle. This *asana* is so-called because in the final pose the hands resemble an eagle's beak.

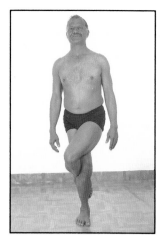  

1 Stand erect, feet joined together. Bend your left knee forward and wrap your left leg around the calf of the right leg, so that the toe of the left foot holds the right leg.

2 Likewise, wrap the left arm around the right one.

3 Join the hands, pointing them like a beak and bend forward. Repeat, alternating the position of the legs and arms.

> *Benefits:*
> Helps to prevent hernia, sciatica, and pain in the knees, shoulders and elbow joints; also useful for those whose job requires them to stand for long hours.

Vrishbhasana

Ox Posture

This is one of the relaxing postures which helps to strengthen the shoulders, thighs and knees. This posture is used to change the *swara* (nasal) breathing.

2 Bring the forearms in front of the knees. The forearms and palms should rest on the ground. Look straight ahead.

3 Reverse this posture to put the body weight on the right thigh with the heel of the right foot touching the anus.

1 Sit on the floor, flexing the legs so that the body weight rests on the left thigh and the foot is under the right thigh. The heels should touch the anus.

> *Benefits:*
> The practice of this *asana* helps stabilise the body and the mind.

Shalabhasana

Locust Posture

This pose is so-called because in its final version the yoga practitioner is balanced on the stomach with the legs and trunk almost vertical—much like a locust. Two variations of the *asana* are given here.

VARIATION I

1 Lie on your stomach with your heels and toes together. Bring your hands below the genitals, crossing your thumbs and interlocking the fingers.

2 Now lift both your legs together, bending the knees, and also the trunk at the same time so that the body rests on the umbilical region. The vision should rest between the eyebrows.

VARIATION II

1 While lying on your stomach keep your hands parallel to the chin on the ground.

2 Lift your hands placing them parallel to the shoulder and stretch them behind you. Simultaneously lift the legs without flexing the knees.

> *Benefits:*
> Besides being useful for backache, lumbago, cervical spondylosis and sciatica, this *asana* helps to relieve constipation and indigestion, and also prevents hernia.

Makarasana

Crocodile Posture

This *asana* is considered a relaxation pose and is used for relieving fatigue. It is also called a *sashtanga dandawata asana* (meaning, to prostrate forward on the ground).

1 Lie on your stomach. Stretch your arms forward, one palm on the back of the other. Join the legs with your toes pointing. The chin rests on the floor. Alternate the position of the palms.

Benefits:
Regular practise of this *asana* prevents diseases related to blood pressure, heart and respiration. It helps young children to gain height and also aids concentration.

Bhujangasana

Cobra Posture

One of the classic poses of yoga which can also be performed by beginners—men, women, children and the elderly alike. The *asana* gets its name from its final pose resembling a cobra, with its hood spread out, ready to strike.

1 Lie on your stomach and chin. Bring the palms near your shoulders, parallel to the chin.

2 Lift the chest and upper part of your stomach away from the floor, while keeping the lower portion of the abdomen on the ground.

3 Lift the body from the genitals upwards, so it rests on the thighs. The gaze is pointed towards the sky.

Benefits:
Helps in backache, cervical spondylosis, indigestion, bronchial asthma and obesity, besides strengthening the tonsils and the thyroid glands.

Person suffering from hernia should not practise this pose.

Yogasana
Yoga Posture

This posture is one of the important advanced, meditative postures. Performing it promotes a sense of stability and balance.

1 Sit in *Padmasana* (see page 16).

2 Bring the left hand round the back and grip the left toe with the left hand. Similarly, grip the right toe with the right hand. The arms are crossed at the back.

3 Bend forward and touch the forehead to the ground. Repeat this pose, alternating the position of the hands. Maintain this pose for the duration that your stamina allows.

> *Benefits:*
> Helps prevent accumulation of fat, hernia. Useful for colitis and asthma. Provides support to the abdominal viscera, prevents constipation and improves digestion.

Ushtrasana

Camel Posture

This posture is among the advanced *asanas*. It stretches the spine and nourishes the spinal nerves. Two variations are given here.

VARIATION I

1 Lie on your stomach and chin.

2 Flex the legs and grip your ankle joints.

3 Now elevate the trunk and legs so that they rest on the lower part of the abdomen and genitals and stretch. Your vision should rest between the eyebrows and breathing should be normal.

Benefits:
Helps in backache, cervical spondylosis, slipped disc, sciatica, as also in diabetes. Prevents accumulation of fat around the stomach and hips; prevents constipation and excess wind-formation.

Ushtrasana:

VARIATION **II**

1 Kneel on the floor.

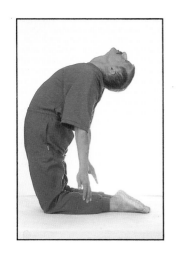

2 Drop your palms on the legs.

3 Bend backwards so as to grasp your heels.

Practise this posture according to your capacity. Persons suffering from blood pressure, heart disease, hernia and prolapsed uterus are prohibited from performing this *asana*.

Chakrasana

Wheel Posture

This *asana* stimulates strong spinal activity, as also blood circulation. Hence its benefit is felt by many glands and organs.

1 Lie on your back. Flex the knees so that the feet rest on the floor. Bend the arms so that the palms are parallel to the neck.

2 Lift the body gradually so it makes an arc.

3 Straighten the elbows and knees as much as possible. The body weight should be on the soles and palms. Lower your body gradually, bringing first the shoulders and then the rest of the body on the ground. Practice *Shavasana* (see page 24) after completing this *asana*.

Benefits:
Useful for backache, diabetes and cervical spondylosis as well as for obesity, this *asana* regulates menstruation, improves height and also helps the muscles supporting the uterus.

Supta Pavanamukt Asana

Supine Wind-Release Posture

This *asana* is so-called because intestinal gases are expelled when the abdomen is squeezed during its performance. There are several variations of the pose, of which one is given here.

1 Lie on your back. Bend your right leg and hold your knee with your left elbow or hands.

2 Bring up the knee to touch the abdomen, holding with both hands. Touch your nose to the knee, raising the head and shoulders and also lifting the left leg about six inches off the ground. Relax and alternate with right leg.

3 VARIATION: Flex both the knees and hold them with both elbows close to the abdomen. The nose should be between the knees. Now roll forward and backward in this pose according to your capacity.

Benefits:
Useful for reducing obesity, hernia, gastric distension, constipation, excessive appetite, indigestion and joint pain.

Persons suffering from backache, cervical or lumbar spondylosis should not practice this *asana*.

Konasana

Angle Posture

This posture is the best known *asana* for bending sideways. It gets its name from *kon*, which means 'angle' in Sanskrit.

3 Bend gradually downwards to the left so that the left hand touches the feet. This may take a little practice, but do not ever bend your knees. Be careful not to bend forward while practising this *asana*.

1 Stand upright, with your legs about three feet apart.

2 Raise your right arm so that the palm faces the ear.

Benefits:
This *asana* makes the waist more supple and helps to reduce fat on the abdomen and shoulders. It is also helpful in backache.

Naukasana

Boat Posture

This posture is so-called because in its final version it resembles a boat. It is a good exercise for stretching the muscles of the chest and abdomen.

1 Lie flat on your stomach and chin. Stretch your arms in front and keep your legs straight and together.

2 Lift the upper portion of your body and your legs simultaneously. Your body should rest on the lower abdomen. Keep your gaze between the eyebrows. Do not hold your breath. Breathe normally.

Benefits:
This *asana* is useful for backache and cervical spondylosis, as well as for bronchial asthma.

Persons suffering from high blood pressure, heart diseases and hernia should not practise this *asana*.

Bandha-Padmasana

Bound-Lotus Position

This *asana* is an advanced variation of the *Padmasana*, a classic meditative pose.

1 Sit in *Padmasana* (see page 16). Cross your arms behind your back and then hold your toes. The back should be absolutely straight and the body should rest on the thighs. Look straight ahead.

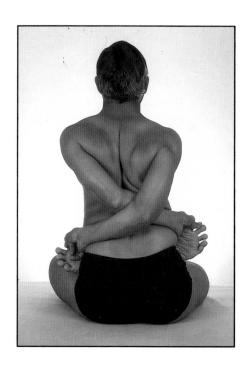

Benefits:
This *asana* stretches the chest muscles and abdomen and is helpful in diseases of the respiratory tract and in preventing diabetes.

Uttanpadasana
Foot-Stretch Posture

Though a posture emphasizing foot-stretching, this *asana* has its maximum effect on the *nabhi-cakra* (navel-plexus), thus reducing most diseases related to a displaced 'navel-centre'.

1 Lie on your back with both the feet together.

2 Bring your arms parallel to the thighs and stretch.

3 Lift the legs as well as arms together so that the body rests on the hip. The nose should be parallel to the toes. Gradually bring the shoulders and feet back on the floor.

Benefits:
Helpful in high blood pressure, hernia, gastric distension and constipation, this *asana* reduces abdominal fat and builds up the chest and breast muscles.

Hasta Padangusthasana

Hand-Toe Posture

Hasta means hand and *padangustha* is big toe. To be able to grasp your big toe with your hand, as in this *asana,* your body must be really supple. Two variations are given here.

VARIATION I

VARIATION II

◄ **1** Stand upright with legs together. Lift the left leg gradually to the side and hold your toe with the left hand. Now gradually stretch the right arm to balance, resting the body's weight on the right foot. Look straight ahead.

1 Lift your left leg in front. ► Hold the left heel with both hands and try to touch the left knee with the forehead. Beginners should take the support of a wall.

Benefits:
Strengthens the calf muscles, helps to improve height and is useful in sciatica, besides helping in concentration.

Ashwathasana

Peepal Tree Posture

This *asana* takes its name from the *peepal* (holy fig) or *ashwath* tree. Like this tree, the pose enables the lungs to draw in more oxygen, which helps improve the respiratory system.

1 Stand upright with your feet together. Stretch your right arm over the head so that the palm faces front. Raise your left arm to be in line with the left shoulder, the palm held downwards.

2 Now stretch your left leg backwards gradually without bending the knees. Balance the body on the right foot. Repeat, alternating the position of the arms and legs.

3 The final Peepal Tree Posture as viewed from the side.

> *Benefits:*
> This *asana* is useful for backache and high blood pressure. Pregnant women practising it will keep fit till the time of delivery as it aids respiration and proper body movement.

Urdhva-Hastottanasana

Up-stretched Arms Posture

One of the important standing *asanas*, the Urdhva Hastottanasana enhances posture and balance as well as increasing physical and mental poise.

1 Stand upright, both feet firmly planted together. Raise your arms overhead and interlock the fingers. The palms should face outwards, the biceps touching your ears.

2 Now gradually bend to the right side and then to the left. Do not bend your knees. Keep your gaze straight in front.

Benefits:
Useful for backache, obesity, and intestinal disorders, the regular practice of this *asana* also helps increase the height in children.

Halasana

Plough Posture

This *asana* is so called because it resembles a plough. It can be practised as a corollary to the Shoulder-stand Posture (*Ardha-Sarvangasana*).

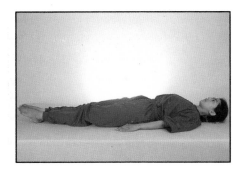  

1 Lie on your back, arms by your side, as in *Shavasana* (see page 24).

2 Lift your legs together gradually and try to move them to the ground behind the head.

3 Try to touch the ground with your toes. Breathe normally. If unable to touch the ground, return to *Shavasana*. After a few months of gradual practice you should be able to achieve the final pose.

Benefits:
This *asana* is helpful in constipation, piles, obesity and diabetes, in diseases of the liver, spleen, skin, eye and the thyroid glands.

Ardha-Sarvangasana

Shoulder-stand Posture

Sarva means 'complete' and *anga* means 'body': hence All-limbs (*Sarvangasana*) Posture is the name sometimes used for this *ardha* (half) posture. The *Ardha-Sarvangasana* is for beginners who may find the *Sarvangasana* difficult.

1 Lie on the back. Keep your arms straight and near the hips as in *Shavasana* (see page 24).

2 Slowly raise both your legs together so as to make an angle of 60° first and then of 90 degrees.

3 Lift your hips with a small jerk and support them with the elbows and back of the upper arms. The body should rest on the shoulders. Come down slowly. Now return to *Shavasana*.

Benefits:
Aiding the flow of blood to the heart and brain, it improves the functioning of the thyroid glands, helps digestion, and strengthens the uterus; also good for obesity and tonsils.

58

Bhunamanasana

Bowing Down Posture

The *Bhunamanasana* is especially recommended for firming the muscles of the hips and waist.
This *asana* is easier for women then men.

1 Sit on the floor, with your legs outstretched and together. Now gradually open them as far apart as you can.

2 Bend forward and try to grasp the right toe with your left hand. Your forehead should touch the knee while the right hand will go to the back. Repeat, alternating sides, 10-12 times.

3 After a few weeks practice, try holding the right toe with the right hand and left toe with the left hand and bend forward so that the forehead touches the floor.

Benefits:
Useful in piles, urinary disorders, and hernia, this *asana* reduces thigh fat, and helps in regulating the menstrual cycle. Helpful in cases of prolapse of the uterus.

Persons suffering from backache, sciatica or cervical spondylosis should not practice this *asana*.

Janu Shirshasana

Knee and Head Posture

In Sanskrit, *janu* means 'knee', and *shirsha* is 'head'; hence this pose is called the Knee and Head Posture.

1 Sit on the ground and stretch your legs forward. Flex the right leg and place the heel near the *umbilicus*.

2 Hold your left toe with both hands.

3 Bend forward so that the forehead touches the knee. The elbows should touch the ground. Repeat, alternating the position of the leg.

Benefits:
Benefits all parts of the body, but is especially useful in hernia and diseases of the testicles. Helpful also for women. It should be practised only under expert guidance.

Persons suffering from backache and sciatica should not practice this *asana*.

Tadasana

Palm Tree Pose

This basic *asana* can be performed by a beginner. Though it looks easy, it is difficult to master for it requires a fine balancing of the body and mind.

1 Stand upright with your toes and heels together. Raise your heels gradually so that the entire body weight is borne by the toes.

2 Gradually raise both your arms, palms facing outwards. Stretch them upwards as if trying to touch the sky. Look straight ahead, resting your vision on any point in front. Hold the pose as long as you can.

Benefits:
Helpful in diseases of the respiratory tract, the joints, and for aching heels and soles. Also aids in concentration. If practised during pregnancy, it facilitates a smooth delivery.

Padahastasana

Forward Bend Posture

Literally, this pose may be called the 'foot-hand posture'. Here, both the feet and hands are united but while standing. This pose strengthens the spine, limbs, abdomen and helps the nervous system.

1 Stand upright with your toes and heels joined together. Raise your arms above your head, with the palms open.

2 Without flexing your knees bend forward and touch the ground with your fingers and if possible with the palms.

3 Now pull back the hands, bringing them parallel to the feet and try to touch your knees with your forehead slowly. Do not bend the knees at all.

Benefits:
Helps youngsters to put on height and aids concentration. Makes the waist supple, reduces hip fat, prevents constipation and improves digestion.

Persons suffering from backache should not practise this *asana.*

Katichakrasana
Lumbar Wheel Posture

The *Katichakrasana*, one of the *asanas* which is useful for both men and women, is also very useful for dancers, as it helps to promote stamina.

1 Stand upright, keeping your feet one-and-a-half to two feet apart. Raise your arms in front of you at shoulder level.

2 Gradually swing leftwards from your waist without changing the position of the feet. Your arms should be parallel to each other.

3 Reach as far back as possible. Keep your gaze on your nose. Repeat, alternating the position of the arms.

Benefits:
Helps to make the waist and ribs supple and is useful in backache, neck pain, high blood pressure, heart diseases, constipation and intestinal disorders.

Supta Vajrasana
Supine Adamantine Posture

This *asana* affects almost all parts of the body. It is considered a highly therapeutic posture in yoga.

1 Sit in *Vajrasana* (see page 19). Bend backwords gradually, taking the support of your elbows and lie down on the ground. Your body weight rests on the feet and head.

2 Extend your arms upwards. Now place the palms parallel to your ears and gradually raise the whole body.

3 Rest your head on the ground and your hands on the thighs. The body weight should be on the head and knees.

> *Benefits:*
> This *asana* is advised for cervical spondylosis, ailments of the thyroid and the para-thyroid, eyes and tonsils; also strengthens the abdominal muscles.

Kagasana

Crow Posture

This pose bears a strong resemblance to a crow; hence the name Crow Posture. Generally, this is the posture practised while performing the *shatkarma* or cleansing process (not indicated in this book), considered basic to yoga.

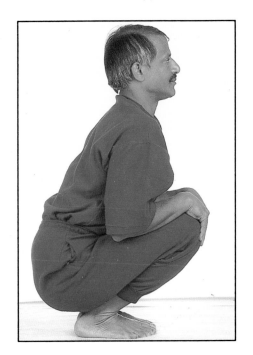

1 Squat on the ground and keep your feet together.

2 Rest your palms on the knees. Keep your neck straight and look in front of you.

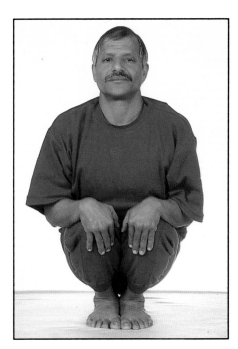

Benefits:
This *asana* makes a person feel more active and helps to balance the body. It is helpful for dancers.

Shirshasana

Head Stand Posture

Considered the 'king of *asanas*', this pose is rejuvenating as it works against the normal pull of gravity on the body. It should, therefore, be practised with caution and step-by-step. Do not rush and try to stand on your head especially after the age of forty.

1 Kneel on the ground, bend forward, rest the forearms on the ground and interlock the fingers. Keep a one foot square cushion on the ground, between the arms, if you find it easier.

2 Now rest the forehead on the ground and gradually stretch the legs so that the maximum weight of the body rests on the arms and head.

3 Flex the knees so that the body rests on the head and forearms.

Benefits:
By rushing blood to the head, this *asana* improves the brain's functioning. It boosts the nervous system and stimulates the endocrine glands.

Shirshasana:

5 After mastering this pose for a few months, try spreading your legs apart, horizontally.

4 After some practice gradually straighten the legs. The body should be at right angles to the elbows.

6 You could also try crossing the legs, while still resting on your head and forearms.

Persons suffering from high blood pressure, heart diseases, sinus and cervical spondylosis should not practice this *asana.*

Ardha-Matsyendrasana
Half Spinal Twist Posture

This *asana* is a simpler version of the *Matsyendrasana* (Spinal Twist Pose) which some may find too difficult to perform. It differs only in that the lower leg rests on the ground, with the heel pressed against the opposite buttock.

1 Sit on the ground and stretch your legs ahead. Flex the right leg and bring the heel close to the left hip. Flex the left knee and bring the left foot behind the right knee.

2 Bring your right arm before the left knee and stretch so as to grip the left foot with the right hand.

3 Stretch out your left arm and bring it around your back so that the body twists to the left side. Repeat the pose, alternating the position of the legs and hands.

4 Back view of the Ardha Matsyendrasana Posture.

Benefits:
As it improves the digestive powers or *jatharagni*, it aids digestion. Also useful for backache, obesity and diabetes.

Karnapeedasana

Aural-Press Posture

This *asana* is a variation of the *Halasana* or Plough Posture. In Sanskrit, *karna* means ear, and *pida* is pressure. As its name implies, the ears get squeezed by the knees in this pose.

1 Lie on your back and practise the *Halasana* (see page 57).

2 Flex the body so that the toes touch the ground at the back of the head.

3 Bend and spread the knees a little. Lower the knees till they touch the ground and hug the ears. The arms should be in the opposite direction to the head, palms facing downwards.

Benefits:
Helps in diseases of the throat (like tonsils), ears and eyes, besides diabetes. It improves digestion and helps prevent gynaecological problems.

YOGA THERAPY

In recent years not solely Ayurvedic practitioners but allopathic medical practitioners too have come to recognize the therapeutic effects of yoga in treating a host of ailments. This is an area which is still being researched. Nevertheless, for diseases like hypertension, heart diseases, diabetes, bronchial asthma, gastro-intestinal disorders, obesity, mental problems, including depression and sleeplessness, sexual impotency, arthritis and spondylosis, yoga has been found to be beneficial.

The yoga treatment includes learning certain cleansing processes or the *shatkarmas*, practising select poses or *asanas*, breathing exercises or *pranayamas* and *mudras* (muscular contractions). The *asanas* are an important part of this whole process, but *must* be accompanied by the other aspects as well for full benefit. Generally, yoga treatment is used as a supplement to other kinds

'[Men] do not understand their own states and actions, or if at all, then only on the surface. It is part of the foundation of yoga to become conscious of the great complexity of our nature, see the different forces that move it and get over it a control of directing knowledge.'

—Sri Aurobindo

of therapies and regimens. Rarely is it used as a treatment by itself.

Many cardiologists in leading hospitals advocate practice of certain *asanas* as part of the regimen to be followed by patients, who have undergone by-pass surgery. They feel that slow, regular practice of these *asanas* over a given period of time helps the patient to recover and consolidate the benefits of a heart by-pass operation.

Yoga has been found to be of great benefit in pregnancy. Practising select *asanas* (given below) helps to exercise abdominal muscles, tones up the system and promotes mental calm, all of which helps in an easy delivery.

Not only adults, but children too can gain from practising yoga. Some *asanas* in particular are not too taxing and help build the muscles, improve height and sharpen concentration, all aspects which are vital for growth in children.

You may wonder why several *asanas* are listed as a therapy for a given kind of ailment. Should you choose one out of them or practice them all? Practising all of them is recommended, but it should be according to your own capacity and suppleness of body. Concessions also have to be made for *asanas* which may be contraindicated for persons suffering from several different ailments; not just the one under consideration for treatment. Yoga draws upon the Ayurvedic concept of the causes of disease. Diseases may have several causes. Besides, the site of origin of a disease may be different from its site of manifestation. For example, asthma, which manifests itself in the lungs, is believed to originate in the digestive system. Thus, *asanas* which strengthen both these organs of the body and can strike at the causes of both the diseases, have to be practised in treating asthma. Moreover, as already mentioned, yoga, like Ayurveda, is a holistic system, which treats body and mind together. The *asanas* selected for certain ailments must ensure this all-round benefit. Thus, it becomes imperative to practice several *asanas* for an ailment. The other processes, namely, *pranayam, shatkarma* (cleansing process), and *mudras* are vital to achieve the mental equilibrium necessary for recovery from an ailment, for good health in general and to reach the ultimate aim of yoga, which is the noble life. (Processes like *pranayam, shatkarma,* and *mudras,* however, are not being dealt with here and the reader may refer to move advanced texts on yoga for instructions on these.)

Supta Pavanmukt Asana

I. HYPERTENSION AND HIGH BLOOD PRESSURE
1. Padmasana (p. 16)
2. Yogasana (p. 45)
3. Gaurakshasana (p. 25)
4. Gomukhasana (p. 22)
5. Ardh-Matsyendrasana (p. 68)
6. Paschimottanasana (p. 27)
7. Simhasana (p. 21)
8. Uttanpadasana (p. 53)
9. Supta Pavanmukt Asana (p. 49)
10. Makarasana (p. 43)
11. Bhujangasana (p. 44)
12. Katichakrasana (p. 63)
13. Tadasana (p. 61)
14. Ashwathasana (p. 55)

II. HEART DISEASE
Excepting acute heart conditions, *yogasanas* and *kriyas* can help in ailments like angina, ischaemia and the like.
1. Padmasana (p. 16)
2. Yogasana (p. 45)
3. Vajrasana (p. 19)
4. Mandukasana (p. 39)
5. Kurmasana (p. 36)
6. Gomukhasana (p. 22)
7. Ardh Matsyendrasana (p. 68)
8. Kagasana (p. 65)
9. Simhasana (p. 21)
10. Paschimottanasana (p. 27)
11. Bhunamanasana (p. 59)
12. Gaurakshasana (p. 25)
13. Padahastasana (p. 62)
14. Guptasana (p. 30)
15. Shavasana (p. 24)

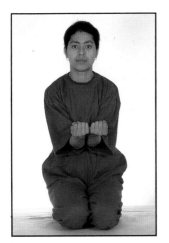

Kurmasana

16. Uttanpadasana (p. 53)
17. Makarasana (p. 43)
18. Katichakrasana (p. 63)
19. Konasana (p. 50)
20. Padhastasana (p. 62)
21. Tadasana (p. 61)
22. Shavasana (p. 24)

III. DIABETES

1. Padmasana (p. 16)
2. Yogasana (p. 45)
3. Uttanpadasana (p. 53)
4. Mandukasana (p. 39)
5. Mayurasana (p. 29)
6. Supta Pavanmukt Asana (p. 49)
7. Ardh-Matsyendrasana (p. 68)
8. Supta Vajrasana (p. 64)
9. Halasana/Sarvangasana (p. 57)
10. Chakrasana (p. 48)

11. Paschimottanasana (p. 27)
12. Bhujangasana (p. 44)
13. Ushtrasana (p. 46-47)

Ushtrasana

14. Konasana (p. 50)
15. Padahastasana (p. 62)

IV. BRONCHIAL ASTHMA AND OTHER RESPIRATORY TRACT DISEASES

1. Padmasana (p. 16)
2. Matsyasana (p. 32-33)
3. Yogasana (p. 45)
4. Bhujangasana (p. 44)
5. Ushtrasana (p. 46-47)
6. Chakrasana (p. 48)
7. Uttanpadasana (p. 53)
8. Sarvangasana/Halasana (p. 57)
9. Vajrasana (p. 19)

10. Mandukasana (p. 39)
11. Supta Vajrasana (p. 64)
12. Gomukhasana (p. 22)
13. Ardh-Matsyendrasana (p. 68)
14. Konasana (p. 50)

Gomukhasana

15. Chakrasana (p. 48)
16. Tadasana (p. 61)
17. Ashwathasana (p. 55)
18. Pranayama

V. GASTRO INTESTINAL DISORDERS

This includes ailments like the irritable bowel syndrome, colitis and chronic constipation.

1. Padmasana (p. 16)
2. Yogasana (p. 45)
3. Vajrasana (p. 19)

4. Simhasana (p. 21)
5. Gomukhasana (p. 22)
6. Mandukasana (p. 39)
7. Kurmasana (p. 36)
8. Supta Vajrasana (p. 64)
9. Ardh-Matsyendrasana (p. 68)
10. Paschimottanasana (p. 27)
11. Uttanpadasana (p. 53)
12. Supta Pavanmukt Asana (p. 49)
13. Halasana (p. 57)
14. Karnpeedasana (p. 69)
15. Bhujangasana (p. 44)

Paschimottanasana

16. Ushtrasana (p. 46-47)
17. Chakrasana (p. 48)
18. Shavasana (p. 24)
19. Urdhva-Hastottanasana (p. 54)
20. Konasana (p. 50)
21. Padahastasana (p. 62)
22. Veerasana (p. 23)

VI. OBESITY
1. Yogasana (p. 45)

Karnpeedasana

2. Paschimottanasana (p. 27)
3. Bhunamanasana (p. 59)
4. Uttanpadasana (p. 53)
5. Supta Pavanmukt Asana (p. 49)
6. Karnpeedasana (p. 69)
7. Bhujangasana (p. 44)
8. Ushtrasana (p. 46-47)
9. Chakrasana (p. 48)
10. Ardh-Matsyendrasana (p. 68)
11. Urdhva-Hastottanasana (p. 56)
12. Konasan (p. 50)

VII. MENTAL DISORDERS
This includes ailments like poor sleep, anxiety neurosis, psycho-neurosis, schizophrenia and maniac depression, loss of memory.
1. Siddhasana (p. 15)

2. Padmasana (p. 16)
3. Muktasana (p. 18)
4. Gaurakshasana (p. 25)
5. Hasta Padangusthasana (p. 54)
6. Ardh-Matsyendrasana (p. 68)

Muktasana

7. Paschimottanasana (p. 27)
8. Halasana/Sarvangasana (p. 57)
9. Shavasana (p. 24)
10. Bhujangasana (p. 44)
11. Chakrasana (p. 48)
12. Shirsasana (p. 66-67)

VIII. SEXUAL IMPOTENCY
1. Siddhasana (p. 15)
2. Guptasana (p. 30)
3. Hasta Padangusthasana (p. 54)

Yogasana

4. Simhasana (p. 21)
5. Ardh-Sarvangasana (p. 58)
6. Gomukhasana (p. 22)
7. Ardh-Matsyendrasana (p. 68)
8. Padmasana (p. 16)
9. Yogasana (p. 45)
10. Sarvangasana/Halasana (p. 57)
11. Bhunamanasana (p. 59)
12. Tadasana (p. 61)
13. Padahastasana (p. 62)
14. Shirsasana (p. 66-67)

IX. CERVICAL AND LUMBAR SPONDYLITIS

Practising *asanas* that entail forward bending is strictly forbidden for persons suffering from spondylosis.

1. Vajrasana (p. 19)
2. Gomukhasana (p. 22)

3. Ushtrasana (p. 46-47)
4. Supta Vajrasana (p. 64)
5. Ardh-Matsyendrasana (p. 68)
6. Padmasana (p. 16)
7. Matsyasana (p. 32-33)
8. Makarasana (p. 43)

Ashwathasana

9. Bhujangasana (p. 44)
10. Shalabhasana (p. 42)
11. Chakrasana (p. 48)
12. Konasana (p. 50)
13. Ashwathasana (p. 55)
14. Katichakrasana (p. 63)

X. NEURO-MUSCULAR DISORDERS

1. Bhadrasana (p. 17)
2. Vajrasana (p. 19)
3. Simhasana (p. 21)
4. Gomukhasana (p. 22)

Shavasana

5. Veerasana (p. 23)
6. Shavasana (p. 24)

XI. GYNAECOLOGICAL DISORDERS

Common among such problems are painful and irregular periods, excessive bleeding, common leucorrhoea, habitual abortion, and prolapse of uterus. Women suffering from a prolapsed uterus should avoid back-bending *asanas*.

1. Padmasana (p. 16)
2. Yogasana (p. 45)
3. Matsyasana (p. 32-33)
4. Vajrasana (p. 19)
5. Mandukasana (p. 39)
6. Supta Vajrasana (p. 64)
7. Gomukhasana (p. 22)
8. Ardh-Matsyendrasana (p. 68)
9. Paschimottanasana (p. 27)
10. Bhunamanasana (p. 59)
11. Gaurakshasana (p. 25)
12. Guptasana (p. 30)

13. Padahastasana (p. 62)
14. Uttanpadasana (p. 53)
15. Supta Pavanmukt Asana (p. 49)
16. Ardh Sarvangasana (p. 58)
17. Halasana/Sarvangasana (p.57)
18. Bhujangasana (p. 44)

Halasana

19. Ushtrasana (p. 46-47)
20. Chakrasana (p. 48)
21. Shavasana (p. 24)
22. Urdhva-Hastottanasana (p. 56)
23. Konasana (p. 50)
24. Padahastasana (p. 62)

XII. YOGA IN PREGNANCY

For each month of pregnancy in the first three months, different *asanas* are recommended.

1st Month

1. Padmasana (p. 16)
2. Yogasana (p. 45)
3. Vajrasana (p. 19)
4. Ushtrasana (Variation II) (p. 47)

Uttanpadasana

5. Gomukhasana (p. 22)
6. Ardh-Matsyendrasana (p. 68)
7. Bhujangasana (p. 44)
8. Uttanpadasana (p. 53)
9. Urdhva-Hastottanasana (p. 56)
10. Konasana (p. 50)
11. Tadasana (p. 61)
12. Ashwathasana (p. 55)

Katichakrasana

2nd Month

1. Padmasana (p. 16)
2. Vajrasana (p. 19)
3. Gomukhasana (p. 22)
4. Tadasana (p. 61)
5. Konasana (p. 50)
6. Ashwathasana (p. 55)
7. Katichakrasana (p. 63)

Konasana

3rd Month

1. Vajrasana (p. 19)
2. Gomukhasana (p. 22)
3. Tadasana (p. 61)
4. Ashwathasana (p. 55)
5. Katichakrasana (p. 63)
6. Konasana (p. 50)

All the *asanas* recommended for the third month of pregnancy can be continued until the sixth month. After the sixth month, only five of the above *asanas—Tadasana, Ashwathasana, Shavasana, Katichakrasana* and *Vajrasana—* should be continued until the last months of pregnancy. It is advisable to lead an active life during pregnancy.

Guptasana

XIII. KNEE AND OTHER JOINT DISORDERS

1. Bhadrasana (p. 17)
2. Vajrasana (p. 19)
3. Sankatasana (p. 28)
4. Kurmasana (p. 36)
5. Garudasana (p. 40)
6. Tadasana (p. 61)
7. Guptasana (p. 30)
8. Paschimottanasana (p. 27)

XIV. INSOMNIA, BLOOD PRESSURE AND ENDOCRINE DISORDERS

1. Katichakrasana (p. 63)
2. Guptasana (p. 30)

Gaurakshasana

3. Siddhasana (p. 15)
4. Bhadrasana (p. 17)
5. Vajrasana (p. 19)
6. Muktasana (p. 18)
7. Gomukhasana (p. 22)
8. Shavasana (p. 24)
9. Gaurakshasana (p. 25)
10. Paschimottanasana (p. 27)
11. Vrikshasana (p. 37)
12. Shalabhasana (p. 42)
13. Shirshasana (p. 66-67)

Janu Shirshasana

XV. URO-GENITAL DISORDERS

1. Gaurakshasana (p. 25)
2. Bhunamanasana (p. 59)
3. Gomukhasana (p. 22)
4. Janu Shirshasana (p. 60)
5. Utkatasana (p. 26)
6. Matsyendrasana (p. 34-35)
7. Garudasana (p. 40)
8. Shalabhasana (p. 42)
9. Katichakrasana (p. 63)
10. Padahastasana (p. 62)
11. Ardha-Sarvangasana (p. 58)
12. Halsana (p. 57)
13. Urdhva-Hastottanasana (p.56)
14. Uttanpadasana (p. 53)
15. Guptasana (p. 30)

PRANAYAMA

(BREATH CONTROL)

Pranayama, the yogic science of breath control, is as essential to Hatha Yoga as the breath is to human life. Smooth deep breathing is an integral part of the performance of many *asanas* and *pranayama* is the technique by which we can train our body for efficacious breathing. *Pranayama* derives from the words 'prana' meaning vital force, and 'ayama' meaning pausing or controlling. *Prana* does not simply mean breath in the limited sense of the term. Apart from the *prana* absorbed from air and food, *prana* stored in large quantities within the body (coiled and latent), are sources of physiological and psychic power which *pranayama* helps to activate. In yogic breathing exercises *prana* is gathered and utilised for tranquilising and stabilising the mind, improving the vital capacity of the lungs, and for a number of respiratory disorders.

The senses {speech, sight, hearing, mind, seed and breath}, when quarrelling together as to who was the best, went to Brahman and said: 'Who is the richest of us?' He replied: 'He by whose departure the body seems worst, he is the richest.'

—Brihadaranyaka Upanishad (155), on the value of yogic breathing.

We normally associate breathing with the dual action of inhaling and exhaling only and are unaware of the brief pauses that occur between the two acts. *Pranayama* divides the act of breathing into four distinct stages, two of which focus on the pause between inhaling and exhaling. The four acts are: (a) *pooraka* (inhaling); (b) *kumbhaka* (a pause in breathing, with full lungs); (c) *rechaka* (exhaling); (d) *bahya kumbhaka* (another pause in breathing, this time on empty lungs).

For the beginner only the first three acts/steps of breathing are indicated as the fourth step should be attempted only under expert supervision. *Pranayama* can be practised in any of the sitting *asanas*, preferably *Padmasana* or *Siddhasana*.

Step 1. *Inhaling:* Sit easily, with the back straight and the head held straight, so that the respiratory muscles are free to expand and recoil comfortably and smoothly. The prime concerns of the practitioner should be *control* on the breathing in of air and on the length of the inhaling process. Breathe deeply, pour air into the lungs. Do not cram so much air into the lungs that it causes discomfort. This could be dangerous.

Step 2. *Suspension:* Hold the breath for the second stage of control. Normally at this stage our respiration is automatically regulated. By suspension of breathing, we are taking over the 'automatic' process of inhaling and exhaling and bringing it under 'manual' control. Do not force yourself and make comfort the criterion. Suspend breathing, but only for a few seconds in the beginning. Regular practise and experiment will disclose your comfortable limits. The longer you have been practising breathing deeply and the more relaxed and poised your sitting position, the more easily will air be retained in the lungs, and an empty pause sustained.

Resist the temptation to let a little air through the nostrils or mouth.

Step 3. *Exhaling:* Let the air out unhurriedly from the lungs. It should slowly begin its ascent through the nostrils. The ease and comfort of the practise should reflect on your face. The more complete and efficient the exhalation, the more efficient the purification of blood cells, and the greater the lung expansion and inflow of fresh air and oxygen in the successive inspiration. Usually twice as much time is allocated to emptying the lungs as to filling them. The time ratio between the three processes to be followed by the beginner are equal, or a little longer for the third step, that is, either 1:1:1 or 1:1:2. The beginner practising *pranayama* on his own should do so once a day, either in the morning or evening, for fifteen or twenty minutes only. *Pranayama* is a complex subject and the reader is advised to refer to a more authoritative book on the subject for the advanced stages of this practise.

Instructions:

1. Inhalation and exhalation should only be of moderate length and for persons with low blood pressure it is advisable to pause briefly after breathing in, but there is no need to make any deliberate pause after breathing out.

2. Practise *pranayama* preferably one hour after the *asanas*.

3. Wear a minimum of loosely fitting clothes. Let four hours elapse from the last meal.

4. Breathe only through the nostrils, unless instructed to the contrary. Breathing through the nostrils is termed Alternate or Sun and Moon Breath. Right nostril breathing is called *Surya Nadi* (Sun Breath), and left nostril breathing is known as *Chander Nadi* (Moon Breath). Left nostril breathing induces coolness in the body while right nostril breathing causes warmth in the body.

5. Practise *pranayama* preferably on a smooth carpet on the ground, in a sitting *asana*.

6. Practice *Shavasana* (see page 24) after *pranayama*.

DHYANA

(MEDITATION)

Meditation *(Dhyana)* is the seventh stage in the practice of yoga. The regular practice of meditation promotes the mind's ability to concentrate. Regular meditation for fifteen to twenty minutes a day can give wonderful results in improving the personality, promoting serenity, and developing a quiet meditative state. In its purificatory function, as in every discipline of yoga, meditation promotes mental hygiene. Meditation calms and tones the nervous system, relaxes and harmonizes psychic energies, recharges psychic batteries and cultivates serenity. In contrast to the external, outwardly focus of attention and energies in our daily lives, meditation obliges us to turn our attention inwards.

Merely sitting still for a fifteen or twenty minute period each day provides mental hygiene of a kind required in yoga. But it must be clear that by 'meditate' in yoga it is

The yogi should try constantly to concentrate his mind on the Supreme Self, remaining in solitude and alone, self-controlled and relieved from desires and longing for possessions.

—Bhagavad Gita

not intended to 'muse or think out' but rather, just the opposite, a suspension of thought, a silencing of the mind's agitation. In the great religions its goal is a knowledge of the Absolute. In the less exalted (but valuable level) the aim may also be relaxation and mental equilibrium.

Although the techniques of yoga meditation are more varied than those of the other esoteric psychologies, some of the basic contemplative exercises in yoga are given below. Meditation is of two types: concentrative and opening up. Yoga mainly utilises concentrative exercises. Patanjali's *Yoga Sutras* teaches that in meditation awareness is to be focused on a fixed point and the mind made steady. This is called concentration or *dharana*.

Concentration is preceded by sense-withdrawal (*pratyahara*), in which internal sounds and sensations take the place of external stimuli. Fix your attention on one thing (*dharana*) without tension, and without any thought for results. The stream of thought should be reduced to one single thought that is the object of your attention. Fix your concentration unflinchingly on this one single object. The object of attention itself is unimportant and may be the most trivial of things. The aim is that of holding a single precept in the mind to still thought entirely. The object you choose may be a flower, a leaf on a tree, a *vase*, Om, clear flame and so on. A small object is preferable to a large one. Exclude all considerations on or about the object, like its size, weight or other qualities. The object is merely reduced to a point where your gaze is steadily fixed, and is kept before the mind as a mere idea. This exercise is called *trataka* or gazing steadily at an object. It may be noted that for regular use meditators often select religious symbols or objects that either have intrinsic beauty or are associated with tranquillity.

The object chosen should be on a level with the eyes, so that there is no strain on the eye muscle. Sit firmly in one of the meditative postures (*Padmasana, Siddhasana*) head, neck and backbone in a vertical line, motionless, breathing slowly and smoothly, and looking steadily at the concentration-object. Do not stare at the object: look *through* the eyes rather than *from* them. Do not stare, or your eyes will soon tire. Blink when necessary, or the eyes will become dry and painful.

In the beginning, you may often find your attention slipping away, and you may be tempted to lapse into a reverie. Whenever this happens bring the beam of your attention back to its object. Simply look. Once concentration comes to be effortlessly sustained, subtler and deeper levels of the mind will be discovered by you.

Each session of concentrative meditation should last fifteen to twenty minutes (ideally both in the morning and evening). You may have to spread your sessions over several months, till you begin to feel the changes in your perception of the object you are focusing on. This change in consciousness is the goal of *dharana* or concentrative meditation.

In steady gaze meditation, after a time the object concentrated upon becomes more vivid and luminous. Sense-withdrawal and concentration aim at triggering a super-conscious state (*samadhi*), which is that of an intuitive realization of the identity of the individual soul and the cosmic soul.

FOOD AND YOGA

'*Yoga is not possible for him who eats too much, nor for him who does not eat at all, nor for him who is addicted to too much sleep, nor for him who is [ever] wakeful, O Arjuna.*'
— *The Bhagavad Gita*

Food is the most important component which nourishes the gross body and subtle mind. It is well known that the state of the mind depends upon the nature of the food taken by an individual. According to Indian concepts the type of foods we eat influences consciousness itself. Three kinds of foods are held to influence human personality: *sattvic* or pure food, *rajasic* or stimulating food and *tamasic* or impure food. Milk, butter, fruit, vegetables and grains are regarded as pure foods; meat, fish, eggs, alcohol and spicy or strong-tasting foods are examples of stimulating foods, as they stimulate the nervous system. Impure foods are all those that are overripe or impure in some way. The corresponding state of consciousness these foods are believed to produce in the mind are spiritual, intermediate and gross respectively. Traditionally, all yogic literature recommends the use of *sattvic* food as it is believed to be alkaline forming, and health depends on a slightly alkaline pH for the bloodstream.

Yoga experts maintain that a growing liking for *sattvic*, wholesome and nourishing food is part of a student's spiritual unfoldment, and that progress in yoga and purity of diet go together.

Eating too much of *rajasic* or stimulating foods causes acid-formation, whose symptoms are lassitude, headache, nausea, insomnia and loss of appetite.

For a modern yoga practitioner, it may be difficult to convert to a purely vegetarian diet, and therefore the following broad directions are given regarding the diet to follow.

1. Take small quantities of food essential for living. Excess food increases laziness and laziness is the biggest enemy of a yogic. The yoga practitioner who takes excessive food is likely to suffer from a number of illnesses and will not achieve the ultimate goal of yoga.

2. Take simple, sweet and lubricated food, enough to just fill half of the stomach. Half the stomach should be kept empty for liquids and gases. The food should preferably be *sattvik,* that is, vegetarian, and ideally, devoid of spices, chillies, onions, garlic, and so on.

3. Take foods rich in milk products.

4. Take freshly cooked food and avoid tinned and junk foods. Also avoid regular use of frozen foods.

5. Avoid excess intake of salty, sour or bitter foods, and also of roasted and fried foods.

6. Do not consume stale food or such food which is reheated.

7. Fresh fruits, vegetables, cereals, grains and so on are suitable foods for the yogi.

8. Bakery products are not encouraged for a yogi, except for leavened breads.

FURTHER READINGS

Brahmachari, Dhirendra, *Yogasana Vijnana*. Asia Publishing House, 1970

Garde, R.V., *Principles and Practice of Yoga Therapy*. Taraporevala, Bombay, 1972.

Hewitt, James, *The Complete Yoga Book*. Leopard Books, London, 1995.

Institute of Naturopathy & Yogic Sciences, *Yoga in Daily Life*, Bangalore, 1995.

Iyengar, B.K.S., *Light on Yoga*. Allen and Unwin, 1966.

————. *Light on Pranayama*. Allen and Unwin, 1981.

Iyengar, Geeta S., *Yoga: A Gem for Women*. Allied Publishers, 1983.

Kumar, Ramesh and Inder Dev Tripathi, *Jayender, Yoga—Prayog*, Megh Prakashan, Delhi, 1982.

Lysebeth, Andre van, *Yoga Self-Taught*. Harper, New York, 1972.

Nagendra, H.R., *Yoga—Its Basis and Applications*. V.K. Yoga, Bangalore, 1994.

————. *Yoga, The Science of Holistic Living*. V.K. Yoga, Bangalore, 1989.

Nimbalkar, Sadashiv, *Yoga For Health and Peace*, Yoga Vidya Niketan, Bombay, 1992.

Sharma, S.K. and Lajpat Rai, *Yoga Therapy in Bronchial Asthma*. Central Research Institute for Yoga, New Delhi, 1994.

Silva, Mira and Shyam Mehta, *Yoga. The Iyengar Way*. Dorling, Kindersley, 1990.

Sinh, Pancham (tr.), *Hatha Yoga Pradipika*, Lalit Mohan Basu, The Panini Office, Allahabad, 1915.

Vasu, Sris Chandra (tr.), *Gheranda Samhita*, Adyar, Madras, 1933.